TOWNSHIP OF UNION
FREE PUBLIC LIBRARY

DISCARD

# JEFF
# GORDON

# JEFF
# GORDON

TOWNSHIP OF UNION
FREE PUBLIC LIBRARY

# ANTHONY B. CAIN
## THE CHILD'S WORLD®, INC.

# ON THE COVER...

Front cover: Jeff talks with crew members at the Daytona 500 in 1998.
Page 2: Jeff raises the trophy after winning the Coca-Cola 600 on May 24, 1998.

Copyright © 2000 by The Child's World®, Inc.
All rights reserved. No part of this book may be
reproduced or utilized in any form or by any means
without written permission from the publisher.
Printed in the United States of America.

Library of Congress Cataloging-in-Publication Data
Cain, Anthony B., 1967–
  Jeff Gordon / by Anthony B. Cain.
      p.    cm.
  Summary: Presents a brief biography and summary of
the accomplishments of NASCAR champion Jeff Gordon.
      ISBN 1-56766-660-4 (lib. bdg. : alk paper)
      1. Gordon, Jeff, 1971–  Juvenile literature.
2. Automobile racing drivers—United States Biography Juvenile Literature.
  [1. Gordon, Jeff, 1971– . 2. Automobile racing drivers.]    I. Title.
      GV1032.G67C35      1999
      796.72'092—dc21      99-19753
          [B]                CIP
                             AC

## PHOTO CREDITS

© AP/Wide World Photos: 2, 6, 16, 20, 22
© Evan Pinkus/SportsChrome-USA: cover
© Greg Crisp/SportsChrome-USA: 19
© U.S. PHOTOGRAPHICS: 9, 10, 13, 15

# TABLE OF CONTENTS

# MEET JEFF GORDON!

Jeff Gordon is a **NASCAR** racecar driver. NASCAR is a name that stands for the National Association for Stock Car Automobile Racing. NASCAR makes the rules for the races. The stock cars used by NASCAR racers have the same shapes and names as American road cars. The racecars have a number on them and are often painted with bright colors. The cars are made to race at almost 200 miles per hour.

In 1998, Jeff won the NASCAR Winston Cup Series championship. He won it by scoring the most points during the year. Racecar drivers are given points depending on what place they finish in the race. The driver who finishes first not only wins the race but also scores the most points. To win the championship, Jeff won 13 of the 34 NASCAR races in 1998.

Jeff holds the Winston Cup trophy
during a celebration on November 8, 1998.

Jeff has always been good at winning races. The Winston Cup Series championship that Jeff won in 1998 was the third of his career. At age 27, Jeff has won many races while competing against the best drivers in the world.

Jeff's success in racing started early and has earned him many nicknames, such as "Wonder Boy," "The Kid," and "Flash Gordon." When Jeff was less fortunate, and had an accident with his racecar, he was even called "Crash Gordon." Whatever people call him, one thing is certain: Jeff Gordon is a great racecar driver.

## GETTING STARTED

Jeff Gordon was born August 4, 1971, in Vallejo, California. He grew up along with his older sister, Kim. Jeff's mother, Carol, married his stepfather, John Bickford, when Jeff was quite young. John was a fan of racing. He took Jeff and Kim to many races.

When Jeff was just four years old, John brought home two *quarter-midget* cars for Jeff and Kim. Quarter-midget racecars are the size of a bathtub and have a three-**horsepower** motor, the same motor as a lawnmower. John took Jeff and Kim to a small racetrack near their house so Jeff and Kim could practice driving the cars. Jeff would drive his car around the track until the motor was too hot to run.

Jeff (in the #4 car, top left) leads the other midget car drivers at Ascot Raceway during a 1990 race.

→

When Jeff was five years old, he entered his first race. Jeff competed in quarter-midget racing at tracks near his home and then raced at tracks all over the country.

In his second year of racing, Jeff won 35 races. He set track records for the fastest speed at five of the racetracks. Two years later, at the age of eight, Jeff won his first quarter-midget national championship. When he won the championship, his parents knew that Jeff had a special talent for driving cars. Jeff continued to race quarter-midget cars for several more years and won the national championship again two years later.

Jeff was nine years old when he started competing in *go-kart* races. The biggest difference between quarter-midgets and go-karts is that go-karts have a 10-horsepower motor. The results of the races were the same. In his first year of competition in the faster, more powerful cars, Jeff won all 25 of the races he entered. Jeff continued to win races and set records racing both quarter-midgets and go-karts. By the time Jeff was 12, he had won three national championships in quarter-midget racing and four championships in go-kart racing.

This little boy is driving the same type of go-kart Jeff drove when he was younger.

# SPEEDING UP

When Jeff was 13, he took his next big step—he began racing *sprint* cars. Larger than the go-karts he was used to, the sprint cars were much faster and more powerful. The engines had up to 700 horsepower, which is twice as powerful as a normal car. After a few times racing the bigger cars, Jeff found driving them to be as easy as driving the quarter-midget cars.

Along with the new car came other changes for Jeff. Jeff would now be racing against adults. Some of the drivers had been driving sprint cars longer than Jeff had been alive. Another change came in the form of new rules. In California, where Jeff lived, it was **legal** for him to race go-karts and quarter-midget cars. However, California laws did not allow Jeff to race sprint cars against adults.

Carol and John Bickford moved their family to Pittsboro, Indiana, in 1986. Indiana laws allow younger people, without drivers' licenses, to race sprint cars. Indiana also had more racetracks and more competition for Jeff. Jeff was racing his sprint car every weekend he could. He continued to win in quarter-midgets, go-karts, and sprint-car racing.

Jeff races in his stepfather's sprint car at Mesa Marin Speedway in 1990. →

## STAYING ON TRACK

During high school, Jeff continued to be successful on the racetrack. He won races and championships driving different kinds of sprint cars. At the age of 19, Jeff was the youngest driver ever to win the United States Automobile Club (USAC) Midget Car Championship. The next year he won the USAC Silver Crown Championship and again was the youngest driver ever to win the award.

## IN THE FAST LANE

Early in 1990, Jeff's racing career took a turn. Jeff went to North Carolina Motor Speedway, a racetrack in Rockingham, North Carolina. A man named Buck Baker has a school at the racetrack where he teaches people how to drive stock cars. Jeff didn't need many lessons. The next year Jeff was racing on the Grand National Series of Stock Car racing. Jeff was named the Series **Rookie** of the Year in 1991.

The following year was even better for Jeff. He moved to North Carolina and continued to do well racing. But more important to Jeff was the day he met Rick Hendrick.

Jeff celebrates after winning the 1990 Belleville Nationals for midget cars in Belleville, Kansas.

Rick Hendrick owns two race teams that compete in the NASCAR Winston Cup Series. The Winston Cup Series is the highest level of stock car racing. Rick had watched Jeff win a race in Atlanta that year and was very impressed with Jeff's driving. Rick offered Jeff the job of driving a new racecar in the Winston Cup Series the following year.

Jeff accepted the offer from Rick. Jeff worked hard the next year and won the 1993 Winston Cup Rookie of the Year award. At the age of 22, Jeff had been racing for 17 years. He had started out with a lawnmower engine on a quarter-midget and was now the best young driver at the highest level of racing.

And 1993 was important to Jeff for another reason. In February, Jeff won a qualifying race for the Daytona 500. That same day he met Brooke Sealey. Brooke and Jeff fell in love and were married the following year.

Jeff and Brooke hold up nine fingers to signal his ninth win of the year on August 30, 1998.

# JEFF GORDON TODAY

Jeff is still racing the car Rick Hendrick owns. You can see Jeff drive the car in Winston Cup Series races. The number on Jeff's car is 24, and the car is painted with the colors of the rainbow. Racing cars in the Winston Cup Series costs a lot of money. Rick has to pay people to work on the car and also has to buy needed car parts. One way in which Rick pays these bills is through **advertising** on the car. Advertisers are called sponsors.

# THE RAINBOW WARRIORS

The people who work on Jeff's car are called the **pit crew.** The crew members work on the motor and change the tires during races. The boss of the crew is called the **crew chief.** Jeff's crew chief is Ray Evernham. Jeff and the crew wear uniforms that have the same advertising as the car. The crew has earned the nickname "Rainbow Warriors" because of their uniforms and the work they do for Jeff.

Jeff Gordon's pit crew scrambles to care for his car during the 1998 Daytona 500.

→

With the help of Rick Hendrick, Ray Evernham, and the Rainbow Warriors, Jeff won the series championship three times in four years from 1995 through 1998. Along with winning 42 races, Jeff has also won over $20 million.

Jeff and Brooke live in North Carolina. They enjoy going to movies and playing video games. Jeff is also involved with several **charities.** He helps raise money for the Leukemia Society of America, and the Make-A-Wish Foundation.

At 27, Jeff Gordon has already achieved a great deal of success. He has won championships at every level of competition. Jeff has also become one of the most recognized racecar drivers in the world. Jeff is not sure what he will accomplish next, but if you want to see him, you might look in the winner's circle.

← Jeff celebrates after winning the Daytona 500 on February 14, 1999.

# TIMELINE

| | |
|---|---|
| August 4, 1971 | Jeff Gordon is born in Vallejo, California. |
| 1975 | Jeff gets his first racecar. |
| 1976 | Jeff competes in his first quarter-midget race. |
| 1977 | Jeff wins the Western States Quarter-Midget Championship. |
| 1979 | Jeff wins the quarter-midget national championship. |
| 1979–1982 | Jeff wins class championships in go-kart racing. |
| 1982 | Jeff wins his second quarter-midget national championship. |
| 1984 | Jeff drives a sprint car for the first time. |
| 1990 | Jeff attends Buck Baker's driving school. |
| 1990 | Jeff becomes the youngest driver to win the USAC Midget Class Sprint Car Championship. |
| 1991 | Jeff becomes the youngest driver to win the USAC Silver Crown Division Championship. |
| 1991 | Jeff moves to North Carolina. |
| 1991 | Jeff is named Busch Grand National "Rookie of the Year." |
| 1993 | Jeff is named Winston Cup Series "Rookie of the Year." |
| 1995 | Jeff wins the NASCAR Winston Cup Series championship. |
| 1997 | Jeff wins his second NASCAR Winston Cup Series Championship. |
| 1998 | Jeff wins his third NASCAR Winston Cup Series Championship. |

 Jeff Gordon leads the pack on his way to winning his second Brickyard 400 on August 1, 1998.

# GLOSSARY

**advertising (AD–ver–ty–zing)**
Advertising is a way of getting people to pay attention to something. The Dupont company pays Rick Hendrick to advertise their paint on Jeff's racecar.

**charities (CHAYR–ih–teez)**
Charities are groups of people who help others in need. Jeff raises money so charities can use it to help people.

**crew chief (KROO CHEEF)**
The crew chief is the person in charge of the pit crew. Jeff's crew chief is Ray Evernham.

**horsepower (HORS–pow–er)**
Horsepower is a way of measuring how powerful something is. Different kinds of racecars have different amounts of horsepower.

**legal (LEE–gull)**
When something is legal, it is allowed by laws or rules. Jeff's family moved to Indiana because it was legal for him to race sprint cars there.

**NASCAR (NAS–car)**
NASCAR is the name made from the first letters of the National Association for Stock Car Automobile Racing. NASCAR makes the rules for auto racing.

**pit crew (PIT KROO)**
A pit crew is a team of people who work on racecars. The crew changes tires and works on the car's motor during a race.

**rookie (ROOK–ee)**
Rookies are people competing in their first year of a professional sport. Jeff was the best rookie racecar driver in the Grand National Series in 1991.

# INDEX

FREE PUBLIC LIBRARY UNION, NEW JERSEY

3 9549 00273 8913

TOWNSHIP OF UNION
FREE PUBLIC LIBRARY

DISCARD

AAW-4809